Sports Illustrated KIDS

STARS OF SPORTS

BRENNA
HUCKABY

PARALYMPIC SNOWBOARDING CHAMP

by Emma Carlson Berne

CAPSTONE PRESS
a capstone imprint

Stars of Sports is published by Capstone Press, an imprint of Capstone.
1710 Roe Crest Drive, North Mankato, Minnesota 56003
www.capstonepub.com

SPORTS ILLUSTRATED KIDS is a trademark of ABG-SI LLC. Used with permission.

Library of Congress Cataloging-in-Publication Data.

Names: Berne, Emma Carlson, 1979– author.
Title: Brenna Huckaby : paralympic snowboarding champ / By Emma Carlson Berne.
Description: North Mankato, Minnesota : Capstone Press, [2021] | Series: Sports illustrated kids
stars of sports | Includes bibliographical references and index. | Audience: Ages 8-11 | Audience:
Grades 4-6 | Summary: "Brenna Huckaby was diagnosed with bone cancer at 14 years old and
had her right leg amputated above the knee. That could have been the end of her sports career.
Instead, the former gymnast took a different route. She fell in love with snowboarding and went
on to become a gold-medal Paralympian. Learn how she overcame obstacles to make it to the top
of the podium in this inspiring biography."—Provided by publisher.
Identifiers: LCCN 2020037721 (print) | LCCN 2020037722 (ebook) | ISBN 9781496695291
(hardcover) | ISBN 9781977153913 (pdf) | ISBN 9781977155665 (kindle edition)
Subjects: LCSH: Huckaby, Brenna, 1996– —Juvenile literature. | Snowboarders—United States—
Biography—Juvenile literature. | Athletes with disabilities—United States—Biography—Juvenile
literature. | Gymnasts—United States—Biography—Juvenile literature.
Classification: LCC GV857.H83 B47 2021 (print) | LCC GV857.H83 (ebook) | DDC 796.939092
[B]—dc23
LC record available at https://lccn.loc.gov/2020037721
LC ebook record available at https://lccn.loc.gov/2020037722

Editorial Credits
Editor: Alison Deering; Designer: Heidi Thompson; Media Researcher: Eric Gohl; Production
Specialist: Spencer Rosio

Image Credits
Getty Images: Alexander Tamargo, 12, 28, Ezra Shaw, 23, Harry How, 13, 22, Maddie Meyer,
19, Mike Pont, 9, Tom Pennington, 16; Newscom: Anthony Souffle/Chicago Tribune/MCT, 18,
Kyodo, 27, Marc Morrison, 11, Mark Reis/ZUMA Press, 26, Mike Blake, 21, Reuters/Jan Woitas/
dpa/picture-alliance, 5, Reuters/Paul Hanna, Cover, Ryu Seung-Il/ZUMA Press, 25, Stephen
Lew/Icon Sportswire, 7; Shutterstock: Felix Mizioznikov, 6, Johnny Adolphson, 15, Mike Peters, 1

All internet sites appearing in back matter were available and accurate when this book was sent
to press.

Direct Quotations
Page 8, from February 23, 2014, *Steamboat Pilot & Today* article, "Leg amputation doesn't slow
cancer survivor's Paralympic dreams," https://www.steamboatpilot.com
Page 15, from International Paralympic Committee profile, https://www.paralympic.org
Page 17, from August 13, 2017, *The Advocate* article, "Losing a leg was only a speed bump in
Brenna Huckaby's athletic road," https://www.theadvocate.com

TABLE OF CONTENTS

Glossary terms are **BOLD** on first use.

GOING FOR GOLD

Brenna Huckaby stared down the dizzying drop of the snow-covered hill in front of her. She was about to compete in the snowboard-cross final of the 2018 **Paralympics** in PyeongChang, South Korea. Beside her stood her competitor and Team USA teammate, Amy Purdy.

Huckaby twisted and stretched, trying to keep her muscles loose in the icy air. She was already a world-champion snowboarder, but this was different. This was her first Paralympic Winter Games.

Huckaby grinned for the camera. Then the official gave the signal. Huckaby gripped the metal handrails beside her. The official shouted, and Huckaby soared down the hill. The race for the gold was on.

<<< Huckaby flies down the mountain during the 2018 Paralympics.

CHAPTER ONE

A YOUNG GYMNAST

Brenna Huckaby has always been an athlete. But she hasn't always been a snowboarder. Huckaby was born on January 22, 1996, in Baton Rouge, Louisiana. It snowed maybe once a year there. No one was skiing or snowboarding.

<<< Downtown Baton Rouge, Louisiana

Huckaby wasn't either. She was busy with gymnastics. She'd been in love with the sport ever since she started training at age eight. Her parents, Jeffry and Kristie, sent Huckaby and her brothers to high school at St. Michael the Archangel. There, Huckaby competed on the gymnastics team. The beam was her favorite event.

⟨⟨⟨ A gymnast competes on beam for the Louisiana State University Tigers.

Huckaby trained hard. She went to competitions and became ranked at a Level 9. Level 10 was Olympic level. She hoped to eventually earn a scholarship and compete in gymnastics at Louisiana State University.

A TRAGIC TURN

But when Huckaby was 13, things changed. Her knee started hurting during gymnastics, mainly when she did the vault. She thought it was probably just a pulled muscle. Early tests at the doctor's office didn't show any injury. So she ignored the pain.

For almost an entire year, Huckaby's knee hurt. Finally, her mother decided they weren't going to ignore the problem any longer.

In 2010, when Huckaby was 14, she and her mother went to the doctor again for another X-ray. Huckaby could tell from her mother's face that something was very wrong. The X-ray showed that a **tumor** was growing. Huckaby had bone **cancer**.

Huckaby was tough. She didn't cry. Instead, she laughed.

"Okay," she said. "What do I do now?"

⟨⟨⟨ Huckaby refused to let her cancer diagnosis slow her down.

CHAPTER TWO

A COURAGEOUS FIGHT

Huckaby and her parents traveled to the MD Anderson Cancer Center in Houston, Texas. It is one of the best cancer treatment hospitals in the United States. Doctors there told Huckaby that she had a type of bone cancer called **osteosarcoma**. She needed treatment—called **chemotherapy**—right away.

Then, doctors offered Huckaby a choice. After treatment, they could try to save her leg, but it would be almost **immobile** for the rest of her life. Or they could **amputate** her leg above the knee.

Huckaby was only 14. She was an athlete. She wanted to try to keep her leg. But chemotherapy wasn't working. The tumor grew from the size of a golf ball to the size of a softball. To save Huckaby's life, doctors had to amputate.

Huckaby's right leg was amputated above the knee on November 18, 2010. She later said it didn't feel real until she woke up. She'd gone into the operating room with two legs. She came out with one and a half.

FACT

Osteosarcoma is often found in children and teenagers. It usually starts in the parts of the bones that are growing quickly, such as bones around the knee.

⟨⟨⟨ MD Anderson Cancer Center in Houston, Texas

A LIFE CHANGE

A month later, Huckaby received her first **prosthetic** leg. After receiving a prosthetic, patients usually use crutches for at least a few weeks—sometimes even months. Huckaby's core strength and fitness helped her. Within a month, she was walking without crutches.

⟨⟨⟨ Huckaby shows off her prosthetic leg at a red-carpet event.

Even as an athlete, **rehabilitation** was hard. Wearing the leg was exhausting. Huckaby didn't have a knee anymore. The muscles and tendons in her hip and thigh had to learn to function in a different way. She had to work for almost a year to build up to wearing her prosthesis all day.

But Huckaby had been competing her whole life. She told herself that recovering from cancer was just a different kind of competition. She would tackle it like any other. And she was determined to win.

⟨⟨⟨ Huckaby uses a different prosthetic leg for snowboarding than she does for walking and running.

CHAPTER THREE
SNOWBOARD
LOVE

In the year after her surgery, Huckaby continued to receive chemotherapy. She also went to **physical therapy**. But she missed gymnastics. When she got back in the gym, though, Huckaby found that her balance was not the same. Her strength was not the same. Even though she tried, she couldn't perform at the same level.

Finally, Huckaby gave up gymnastics. Her body was different now. The sport no longer felt like a good fit. She tried other sports, including swimming and water-skiing. Nothing clicked.

FACT

Park City, Utah, was the site of the snowboarding competition during the 2002 Olympics. The Park City Mountain Resort has the most skiable and boardable landscape in the United States.

In December 2011, Huckaby was invited to go on a special ski trip to Park City, Utah. This trip was organized by the MD Anderson Cancer Center. It was specifically for kids who had lost limbs.

"I had never seen a big mountain with snow on it, or a ski resort before my amputation," Huckaby said.

⟨⟨⟨ Ski and snowboard runs in Park City, Utah

Huckaby couldn't wait to try snowboarding. But first she had to convince the **chaperones** from MD Anderson. Amputees weren't usually allowed to snowboard on their first trip. The adults didn't know if Huckaby was strong enough to make it down a slope. They didn't know if her balance was good enough.

Huckaby didn't either. But she wanted to try. She fought for the chance to go down the slopes. Eventually, she convinced the adults.

⟨⟨⟨ Huckaby flies down the mountain during a Dew Tour event in 2018.

A new world opened as Huckaby soared down the slopes. She loved the freedom and the movement. She loved the snow spraying up into her face. After her first run, Huckaby came off the mountain with her eyes shining. She was hooked.

Following that first trip, Huckaby began snowboarding regularly. Her family took ski and snowboard trips during school breaks. The snowboard reminded Huckaby of a moving balance beam. And the beam had once been her favorite event.

Love of the Slopes

Huckaby has explained how her gymnastics training helped her make the move to snowboarding. "I think my gymnastics background is what has made me so successful," she said. "I use my balance all the time in snowboarding. Air awareness, body awareness, that is so crucial in what I do, and I have been training since I can remember in gymnastics, so it kind of translated over so easily."

CHAPTER FOUR

TRAINING TIME

Soon, Huckaby learned about para-sports competitions. They are for athletes with physical disabilities. Huckaby realized she could become a para-snowboarder. She could go all the way to the Paralympic Games.

‹‹‹ The National Ability
Center in Park City, Utah

⟨⟨⟨ Huckaby celebrates after a win.

Huckaby remembers this decision as a turning point. She'd always competed athletically. That was how she spent her time. Since losing her leg, it was a hole that needed to be filled. And now she had a way to do it.

In 2013, Huckaby moved to Utah with her mother. She began training at the National Ability Center. The center focused on introducing athletes with physical disabilities to outdoor sports.

Just three years after her amputation, Huckaby was ready to begin her para-snowboard training. The Paralympics were in her sights.

COLLECTING MEDALS

Huckaby began competing in 2013. The following year, she traveled to Copper Mountain, Colorado, to compete in the U.S. Paralympics Snowboard Cross National Championships. She was still new to the sport but landed a bronze medal.

Huckaby kept training and racing. In December 2014, she learned she had made the U.S. Paralympics Snowboarding National Team. She would be competing at the international level.

In February 2015, the U.S. Paralympics sent eight athletes to La Molina, Spain. They were there for the IPC Para-Snowboard World Championships.

Huckaby was one of the athletes. She was going to her first world championship. Many eyes would be watching. Huckaby did not disappoint. She took home a gold medal in snowboard cross and a silver in banked slalom.

Para-Snowboard Events

Paralympic snowboarders compete in two events—snowboard cross and banked slalom. In snowboard cross, a group of snowboarders races around obstacles. In banked slalom, one athlete competes at a time. The course features even tighter turns. Athletes race a course three times. Their fastest time wins.

⟨⟨⟨ Huckaby joined Team USA in 2014.

A TRIUMPHANT RETURN

Huckaby returned to the IPC Para-Snowboard World Championships in 2017, this time in Big White, China. At age 21, she was ready to face down her biggest **rival**, French snowboarder Cécile Hernandez-Cervellon. The two competed against each other in snowboard cross.

Hernandez held the lead until the second-to-last run of the race. Then Huckaby saw her chance. She moved to the inside of one of the turns. It was just enough. She finished the course in one minute, 16 seconds—two seconds faster than Hernandez.

The next day, Huckaby clocked the fastest time in her second banked slalom run to win another gold. She claimed two gold medals in total at the 2017 championships. Huckaby was now one of para-snowboarding's top athletes.

⟨⟨⟨ Huckaby's official Team USA portrait for the 2018 Paralympics

Huckaby competes in banked >>>
slalom in Colorado in 2018.

CHAPTER FIVE
SNOWBOARD CHAMPION

After becoming a world champion, Huckaby was ready for her biggest competition yet. She traveled with Team USA to the 2018 Paralympic Games in PyeongChang, South Korea.

There, she faced off against American Amy Purdy in the snowboard cross final. Purdy was already an experienced snowboarder. She had won bronze in snowboard cross at the 2014 Winter Paralympics in Sochi, Russia. Huckaby was still new to the sport. These were her first Paralympics.

At the signal, the two women pushed out of the gates and soared down the hill. Huckaby took the lead almost immediately. She matched her body to each jump. She stayed as close as possible to each gate. The farther away she moved, the longer her run would take. Huckaby had gold in her sights. But could she beat her teammate?

Huckaby catches air on the slopes. 〉〉〉

GOLD-MEDAL WINNER

Huckaby and Purdy skidded down the slopes. They pinwheeled their arms for balance. Both boarders pushed their limits to gain just a few seconds of extra time.

As Huckaby soared over the last big jump to the finish line, her board hit the snow in a perfect landing. Purdy was well behind her. Huckaby had won the very first gold medal of the 2018 Paralympic Games!

⟨⟨⟨ Huckaby tears down the hill at the PyeongChang Winter Paralympic Games.

⟨⟨⟨ Huckaby took home gold in her first
trip to the Paralympic Games.

Four days later, she would win another. Huckaby
raced against Purdy and Hernandez in banked slalom.

Purdy came in third with a time of 1:05:40.
Hernandez won silver with a time of 56:53. Huckaby's
best time was 56:17. She came in first and brought
home the gold. It was official. Huckaby was now the
best female para-snowboarder in the world!

LIFE OFF THE BOARD

Huckaby has a life off the slopes too. In June 2019, she married fellow snowboarder Tristan Clegg. They already had a daughter named Lilah. In early 2020, their second daughter, Sloan, was born.

Huckaby hopes to get a college degree in special education. She has recently started a YouTube channel to explain what amputee life is like. And she's looking ahead to the 2022 Paralympics in Beijing, China. She's determined to own the slopes again.

TIMELINE

1996 Brenna Huckaby is born on January 22 in Baton Rouge, Louisiana.

2010 Huckaby is diagnosed with osteosarcoma and has her right leg amputated at MD Anderson Cancer Center in Houston, Texas.

2012 Huckaby discovers snowboarding on a rehabilitation ski trip organized by the MD Anderson Cancer Center.

2013 Huckaby moves to Utah to train at the National Ability Center in Park City.

2014 Huckaby enters her first para-snowboard race and comes in third.

2015 Huckaby takes home gold and silver medals at the 2015 IPCAS Para-Snowboard World Championships.

2017 Huckaby competes again at the 2017 IPC Para-Snowboard World Championships and wins two gold medals.

2018 Huckaby wins two gold medals at the 2018 Paralympic Winter Games in PyeongChang, South Korea.

GLOSSARY

AMPUTATE (AM-pyuh-tayt)—to cut off someone's arm, leg, or other body part, usually because the part is damaged

CANCER (KAN-suhr)—a disease in which some cells grow faster than normal and destroy healthy organs and tissues

CHAPERONE (SHAP-uh-rohn)—a person who goes with and is responsible for a group of young people

CHEMOTHERAPY (kee-moh-THER-uh-pee)—a type of cancer treatment in which cancer cells are destroyed with drugs

IMMOBILE (ih-MOH-buhl)—unable to move or be moved

OSTEOSARCOMA (OS-tee-oh-sahr-KOH-muh)—a type of cancer of the bone

PARALYMPICS (pa-ruh-LIM-piks)—a series of international competitions for athletes with physical disabilities

PHYSICAL THERAPY (FIZ-uh-kuhl THER-uh-pee)—the treatment of diseased or injured muscles and joints with exercise, massage, and heat

PROSTHETIC (pross-THET-ik)—an artificial body part that takes the place of a body part, such as an arm or leg

REHABILITATION (ree-huh-bil-uh-TAY-shun)—therapy that helps people recover their health or abilities

RIVAL (RYE-vuhl)—someone whom a person competes against

TUMOR (TOO-mur)—an unhealthy mass of cells in the body

READ MORE

Chandler, Matt. *Declan Farmer: Paralympic Hockey Star.* Mankato, MN: Capstone Press, 2021.

Derr, Aaron. *Sports of the Paralympic Games.* South Egremont, MA: Red Chair Press, 2020.

Herman, Gail. *What Are the Paralympic Games?* New York: Penguin Workshop, 2020.

INTERNET SITES

Brenna Huckaby, International Paralympic Committee
www.paralympic.org/brenna-huckaby

Brenna Huckaby, Team USA
www.teamusa.org/para-snowboarding/athletes/Brenna-Huckaby

What Is Cancer?, KidsHealth
kidshealth.org/en/kids/cancer.html

INDEX